CONTENTS

The Projects

INTRODUCTION

This book is a celebration of making books with children over a six-year period.

As part of my research, I compared children's work in the book arts with their other writing and artwork. What was discernible was that writing tasks were more successfully completed when children were engaged in the production of books than with other vehicles for writing. Children learned that texts are constructed differently when enhanced by accompanying illustrations and disciplined by the size and orientation of the page.

The sense of ownership was overwhelming. 'When can we take our books home?' was a constant cry. One girl was so adamant that she wanted all her books returned that she insisted that I take apart the group books her work was in so that her contributions could be reclaimed! Similar requests came from parents. Can you imagine responses like this to work in an exercise book?

Only a book several times the size of this could do justice to an analysis of all that was produced during this time of making books. Here, the focus is on how to make just a few of them, using for the most part basic paper-folding and scissor-cutting techniques. There are no limits to the variety of writing, design and illustration styles that these book forms can be used for. To inspire you, I have outlined the projects that I set for children, but remember that you can mix and match book forms with themes, or adapt the ideas to suit your own classroom or home.

I hope teachers, parents and children will find the book forms described here exciting to make and a stimulus par excellence for acquiring the highest of standards in writing.

Paul Johnson

A pop-up butterfly card by Christopher (age 6)

4

Making Books

Paul Johnson

Reprinted 2005
First published in 2000 by
A & C Black Publishers Limited
37 Soho Square, London W1D 3QZ
www.acblack.com

ISBN-10: 0-7136-5077-X
ISBN-13: 978-0-7136-5077-8

Copyright text and illustrations © 2000 Paul Johnson
Photographer: Zul Mukhida
Literacy Consultant: Christine Moorcroft
Editor: Claire Watts

The author and publisher would like to thank the staff and
pupils of Beaver Road Junior and Infant School, Didsbury,
Manchester, for their help with this project.

A CIP catalogue record for this book is available from the
British Library.

Printed in China by WKT Co. Ltd.

The Book Art Project runs courses in developing
children's writing through the book arts. For details of
courses and publications, contact Paul Johnson at:
The Book Art Project, 11 Hill Top Avenue, Cheadle Hulme,
Cheshire SK8 7HN
Tel: 0161 485 2174   E-mail: bookart@btinternet.com
www.btinternet.com/~bookart/

A carousel book by Mariana (age 7)

MAKING BOOKS AND THE CURRICULUM

The projects in this book are designed to develop children's skills in literacy while they learn about other subjects. They cover a range of fiction and non-fiction genres, each demanding different combinations of skills at text, sentence and word level. Children then use these literacy skills to help them learn more about other subjects. Teachers can combine work in English, design technology and art with subjects such as science, history and geography.

Project	Range	Text-level skills
1, 2, 4, 5	Fiction: stories with predictable structures and familiar settings	Using print to tell stories. Understanding that writing always says the same thing and that it is written in a particular direction. Distinguishing between writing and drawing. Experimenting with writing. Thinking about, planning and discussing what to write. Making simple picture books with sentences modelled on basic text conventions and learning vocabulary about books: 'cover', 'author', 'title', 'layout'. Building simple profiles of characters. Using the language of time (for example, 'when', 'suddenly', 'after that'). Identifying and describing characters.
3, 9	Stories and poems with familiar settings, traditional stories and poems, those from different cultures, humorous stories and poems	Discussing story settings. Developing awareness of authorship and publication. Using story settings from reading in their own writing. Learning, collecting, re-reading and responding imaginatively to favourite poems. Making collections of humorous stories and poems. Using structures from poems as a basis for their own writing.
6, 7, 8, 10	Information books	Distinguishing between fact and fiction. Writing non-chronological reports.
11	Plays	Being aware of different voices in drama. Recognising the differences between prose and playscripts. Writing dialogue.
12, 13	Traditional stories	Stories by significant children's authors. Identifying story themes. Identifying and discussing main and recurring characters. Writing portraits of characters. Writing alternative sequels for stories.
14	Adventure stories and traditional stories	Planning main points as a structure for story-writing. Describing and sequencing key incidents. Re-telling the main points of a story in sequence. Plotting a sequence of episodes modelled on a known story.
15, 17, 20	Persuasive writing, advertisements and flyers	Summarising. Designing an advertisement, using design and linguistic features learned from reading examples. Considering the audience, context and purpose of a text.
16	Poems on a theme	Comparing and contrasting poems on similar themes. Writing poems on personal experiences.
18	Short novels	Writing character sketches.
19, 28	Reports, information books and non-chronological reports	Identifying features of non-fiction books: content, structure, vocabulary, style, layout and purpose. Writing non-chronological reports. Researching: reviewing, collecting information, scanning, making notes. Presenting a non-fiction text: using pictures and diagrams.
21, 27	Persuasive leaflets and arguments	Collecting and analysing the persuasive devices. Writing arguments to persuade others of a point of view.
22	Diaries	Recognising the effect on the reader of the choice between first and third person. Writing in the first person.
23	Recounts of events	Identifying the main features of recounted texts. Writing recounts based on a topic or personal experience.
24, 25	Stories by significant children's writers	Analysing the features of a good opening and experimenting with different ways of opening a story. Mapping out texts showing development and structure.
26	Instructional texts and information books	Writing instructional texts based on personal experience.
29, 30	Non-chronological reports and reference texts	Writing a brief synopsis of a book for a cover blurb.
31	Observations which recount experiences; journalistic writing.	Understanding the features of non-chronological reports. Developing a journalistic style.

ABOUT THIS BOOK

Many of the best children's books today are true masterpieces of design, with imaginative texts, pop-ups, pull-outs and removable items to stimulate young, enquiring minds. But with such sophisticated models, can the gap between what children read and what they write be narrowed at all? *Making Books* sets out to achieve this aim, by showing how children, even as young as five, can combine words, images and paper-engineering to make books just like those they delight in.

Story-writing is given a special place here, but descriptive and analytical writing is embraced too. There is a poetry project, a historical project and several projects which focus on quite different writing styles, such as brochures, advertising flyers and invitations.

Teachers should be able to pick any project from this portfolio of book-making ideas and adapt it to their curriculum planning. There is no reason why one book form should not be used as the foundation for the writing project described in another, or why a book form designed for five-year-olds should not be made by top juniors.

The book projects

The projects are roughly in the order in which I originally introduced them to children, starting with the youngest and finishing with the oldest. You could successfully use a project from any part of the book to introduce children to book-making. However, working through several projects (starting with one of the simpler forms) will help children to gradually develop their book-making skills, so that they can look back at their first creations and clearly see the progress they have made.

At first, young authors will write directly into their books. In time, children should be able to draft and redraft pages, checking grammar, punctuation and spelling and the factual accuracy of their writing. They will learn to judge the value of illustrations and diagrams within the text and be able to stand outside their writing and respond to it as critical, independent readers.

'The Cat and the Dragon' by Sarah (age 6)

How the book project pages work

To help with planning, all the projects are arranged under the following headings:

AGE 5–6 gives the age-group for which the project was designed. Simpler book forms can be easily combined with other themes for older pupils, while more complex book forms can be made by younger pupils with more assistance.

AIM describes the book form and project theme.

PREPARATION tells you which parts of the book-making were done by the children and which parts I did in advance. (Sometimes I did more preparation, not because children were incapable of doing these things, but to speed up the activity.) This section also suggests the approximate length of time to allow for the project.

How to use this project suggests how you might organise the project in the classroom and offers ideas about how to use the book forms.

How to make the book shows you how to construct each book form with simple step-by-step instructions and illustrations.

MORE IDEAS offers suggestions for extending, simplifying or varying the project.

Some projects also include other simple paper-engineering ideas and design tips to help children create better books.

BASIC BOOK FORMS

When children begin book-making, talk them through each folding action, step by step. Practise with junk mail or copy paper.

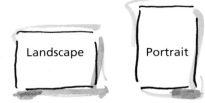

Landscape   Portrait

Hold a sheet of paper against the wall in landscape position, and have each child copy your movements with his or her paper. Explain your steps as you fold:
1. Take the right edge to the left edge, making sure the corners touch.
2. Press the edges together with your left hand.
3. Now put your right hand next to your left hand and smooth across the paper to the middle of the fold.
4. Flatten the paper there. Then flatten the paper up to the top of the sheet and down to the bottom. Your paper should now be folded neatly in half. (You will need to modify instructions for left-handed pupils.)

How to make a concertina book

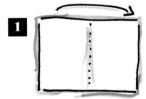

1

2

With the paper in landscape position in front of you, fold the left edge to the right edge, then open out.

Fold the left and right edges to the centre and open out.

3

4

You now have four vertical panels.

Fold the top edge to the bottom.

5

Fold the left edge forward along the first crease. Continue folding along the creases in a zig-zag.

How to make an origami book

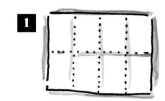

1

2

Follow the instructions for a concertina book to stage 4. Unfold the paper to reveal eight rectangular panels.

Fold the left edge to the right edge. Cut through the centre of the fold along the crease to the next vertical crease.

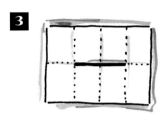

3

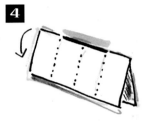

4

Open out the sheet to reveal a slot in the centre.

Fold the top edge to the bottom edge.

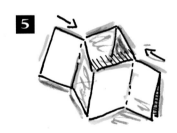

5

6

Push the left and right edges towards the centre to form a cube.

Continue pushing the edges to the centre, to make a cross.

7

Take two adjacent pages and fold them around all the other pages. Crease the spine and the edges of the pages thoroughly.

PLANNING BOOKS

Before writing

The 'warming-up' period prior to writing is very significant. This is a time when characters are brainstormed, plots discussed and possible story resolutions improvised. In some contexts, such as a factual study, it may be useful to have a pre-writing session several days or weeks ahead of the project in order to generate ideas. By planning ahead, children will be better prepared for the task of drafting the book when the time comes.

Making storyboards and page plans

With short, simple books, it is often useful to plan using a visual storyboard (see page 13). With more complex books, a page plan that lists headings and illustrations on each page is helpful (see page 53).

Drafting

Usually children need to write a draft of their text on scrap paper before writing it on the finished page. Supply, or have children make, a card template about one centimetre smaller than the book page. Children draw round this in the centre of their draft pages and also in the centre of their finished book pages. This will ensure that the drafting is done in the same area as the work presented in the final book.

Draft pages

Finished book

Card template

Working patterns

There are many ways to tackle each project, but it is best to try to keep all the children working the same way. One child in my junior class insisted on writing directly into the book without drafting. Her books, not surprisingly, were a mass of grammar and spelling errors but she wrote with a consistency and originality that was unmatched by her peers. I suggest you plan to stick to one of these patterns:

● Children draft the whole text, write it in the book, then add the illustrations.

● Children complete one written and illustrated page or spread at a time.

● Children make all the illustrations in the book, then use these as reference and stimulation for the text.

Although young children have limited concentration spans, I find that they have little difficulty in continuing for several weeks on a specific project. Only knowledge of individual children can determine when more can be expected of them, or when they have had enough of a particular project.

Using computers

Computers can be invaluable for children's planning and presentation of text and graphics. However, I would advise in favour of handwritten and drawn work. Most professional children's illustrators prefer pencils and brushes to computer-generated images. And only pen-to-paper writing or drawing can ensure that the whole class is engaged on the same activity simultaneously.

Publish your own books

Basic book forms (see page 7) can be opened flat, laid on a photocopier and reduced to A4, allowing you to produce a limited edition of a book. It was my own practice to limit children to one photocopy-printed book per term.

EVALUATION

These pointers are designed to help teachers evaluate children's achievements.

At the infant stage

In acquiring literacy, consider how children are faring in:

- understanding what a book is;
- comprehending how pages are linked together;
- linking words and pictures;
- creating stories or rewriting known ones;
- acquiring basic writing skills.

As illustrators, designers and technicians, consider how children are faring in:

- learning to draw from observation;
- handling different kinds of drawing materials with confidence;
- folding paper in half;
- using scissors.

Socially, consider how children:

- share their own books with their peers;
- discuss story developments with their partners;
- show willingness to read their books to the class.

At the junior stage

In acquiring literacy, consider how children are faring in:

- planning the contents of a book;
- drafting and editing texts;
- conceiving a text for a specific audience;
- developing grammar, punctuation and spelling skills.

As illustrators, designers and technicians, consider how children are faring in:

- designing a page spread in different ways;
- pictorial composition;
- matching illustrations to text;
- folding, cutting and assembling books;
- planning pages into designed areas.

Socially, consider how children:

- collaborate with a partner or in a team;
- give criticism and advice;
- take criticism and advice.

Planning future book art projects with all ages

- What did the children generally find hardest?
- With which part of the process did children seem most involved?
- How many finished their books in a given time period? If the collective answer is less than 50 per cent, how might the rate be improved?

Keeping Personal Records

Compiling a personal critique of likes and dislikes, strengths and weaknesses provides children with an individual record of the books they have made. It is also a useful indicator for the teacher of how children perceive their skills and of what strategies are needed to improve standards. Children can use the Personal Record Book (page 64) to review and evaluate their own books. This sheet can be photocopied up to A4, then folded, cut, and refolded following the origami book assembly instructions (see page 7).

TIPS FOR SUCCESSFUL BOOK-MAKING

Creating book illustrations

● Children draw their partners in a relevant pose. The artist then becomes the model for the posing child.

Lennard (age 10) drew this picture of his partner.

● Make card figures which children can arrange in the position required for illustrations of people. Join the limbs with paper fasteners.

● An object can stand out in an illustration or recede into a 'warm' or 'cool' background. Encourage children to discover this for themselves by limiting their palette to just one or two colours for an illustration.

● A sketchbook is invaluable for making random sketches or careful studies. These can be 'made to order' for a specific book illustration or amassed for reference like a scrapbook.

Organising illustrations

It can take much longer to illustrate a story than to write it, so delegate time for each activity as follows:

● Children use colour in only one of every five books they make. The rest are written and illustrated in pencil or ink.

● One book per term is an essentially visual one while others emphasise writing.

● Illustrations are made directly into books (or on sheets of paper glued into books), and not 'drafted', as with writing.

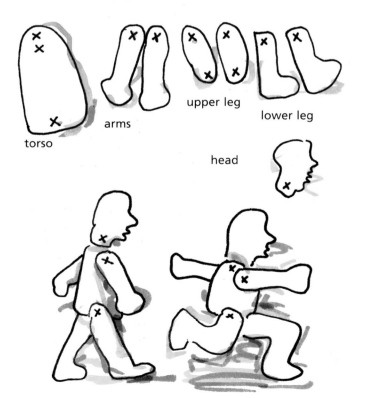

torso

arms

upper leg

lower leg

head

There are all kinds of ways to position illustrations.

Designing book covers

● Divide book covers into three parts: title, author's name and artwork.

● Discuss ways of making covers exciting, such as drawing the most dramatic part of the story.

The cover to Christopher's picture book (age 5)

● Using classroom picture books, show children different kinds of lettering, such as italic, bubble or serif lettering.

● Encourage chidren to write back cover 'copy'. This could include a 'blurb' to sell the book, a synopsis, a publisher's logo, details about the price and an invented barcode.

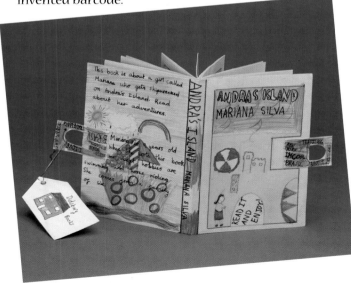

'Andra's Island' by Mariana (age 9). A luggage label adds the finishing touch to a suitcase-shaped cover.

Safety Procedures

Using scissors

● To stop scissors becoming a safety hazard, make sure they are never hidden under sheets of paper. When not in use, place them in the closed position at the top of the table, ideally in a scissors rack.

● Children should draw pencil lines showing where cutting is to be done so that they can hold the paper well away from this area.

Using a craft knife

● If using a retractable blade, expose it by approximately 3 cm.

● Use a safety ruler to cut along and cut on a mat.

● Ensure that the hand holding the paper is always behind the knife.

● When cutting, hold the knife horizontally and avoid pointing the blade downwards.

Materials

Paper

'A' sized papers are standard in school suppliers' catalogues. Paper sizes suitable for making books range from A1 (594 x 840 mm) to A4 (297 x 210 mm). A3 (420 x 297 mm) is an ideal size for making concertina and origami books.

Use newsprint, packaging paper or A4 copy paper to make trial runs of book forms. For finished books, cartridge (drawing) paper around 120 gsm in weight is recommended.

Glue

PVA glue is recommended for most book-making. However younger children may find it easier to use a glue such as Pritt Stick®.

1 · TOY STORIES I

 AGE 5–6

AIM: To create a concertina-style picture book with four pages.

PREPARATION: I duplicated sheets to make a book for each child with an illustration frame on each page.

🕐 Allow about three 1-hour sessions.

How to use this project

Improvise a narrative with the class using a toy animal as the main character. Encourage children to join in by asking questions and making suggestions. Focus on words which say what the character does in the story: hides, jumps, plays, runs, walks and so on. Go back over the story scene by scene and have children draw each scene into the frames, writing captions above or below the illustrations. Extra pages could be added to extend the story.

Children could use folded card to make covers for their books. To attach the book, make a 1 cm fold on the edge of the first page and glue it inside the cover.

How to make the book

1

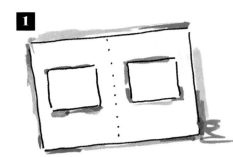

Fold a sheet of A4 paper in half. Draw a black box frame in the centre of each panel on one side of the paper. This is your master copy.

2

Duplicate the master sheet twice for each child. Align the short edges and tape them together to make a concertina book.

DESIGN TIP

● Make the frames more interesting by adding a decorative border.

In this book, Ciera (age 5) tells a story about a cat in four simple captions.

2 · TOY STORIES II

AIM: To create a four-page folded picture book.

PREPARATION: I drew the frames on one sheet, photocopied it and folded the copies to make a book for each child.

 Allow two 1-hour sessions.

How to use this project

Share a story with the class, then cover up the words. Ask the children to describe what is happening in each picture in simple sentences. Write these on strips of paper. Place the sentences beneath the pictures and compare them with the original.

Show the children some toys to give them inspiration for their own books. They could draw a different doll or toy in each of the four illustration frames and simply label each picture, or make up a story about one character.

Christopher (age 5) tells the story of Daren who sleeps under the bed and eats his breakfast with a knife!

How to make the book

1 Fold A4 paper in quarters. Draw a frame in each panel. With the paper lying landscape, cut along the left horizontal crease to the centre.

2 Turn the sheet over and draw two frames on the cut side.

3 Fold the paper in half lengthways so that four frames are showing.

4 Fold the loose panels around the other pages to make a four-page book.

MORE IDEAS

Storyboards

Children could plan their books using a storyboard. To show them how, draw six boxes on A4 paper and write a sentence under each. Copy the sheet and ask children to illustrate each sentence. Then children can draw a storyboard for their own books.

Cut-out Book

Children who need additional support could cut out pictures from a story in a comic and sequence them. Beneath each picture, they could write a sentence, perhaps using some of the words of the original.

3 · POP-UP BOX BOOK

> **AIM: To make a simple pop-up story book.**
>
> **PREPARATION:** I made the basic pop-up box book for each child.
>
> Allow a 1-hour session for each of the three spreads.

How to use this project

Show children a book with simple pop-up shapes. Talk about which parts of the story have been chosen to pop-up on each page. Is the pop-up the main theme of the page? Is it something surprising that appears or happens in the story? Discuss what the cube-shaped pop-ups in the pop-up book form could represent. Ideas might include a TV screen, a shop or a gift-wrapped present. What other suggestions can children come up with? As a class, weave a story around the pop-up ideas. Children can write and illustrate their own version of the class story, or make up a new one of their own.

Oliver (age 5) has turned the book on its side and used the pop-up to represent a house in his story 'Crocodile's House'.

How to make the book

1
Use A3 paper to make an origami book to stage 3 (see page 7).

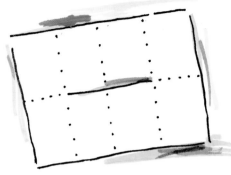

2
Fold the left and right edges to the centre. Cut two parallel slits in three of the panels, as shown.

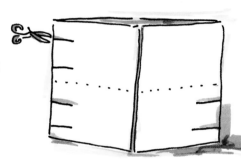

3
Fold each middle section upwards to make a flap.

4
Unfold the flaps and open out the paper.

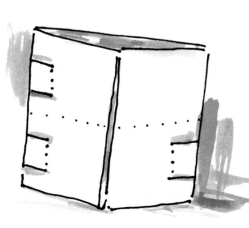

5

Fold into an origami book, making sure all the pop-up sections are on the inside pages.

6

Open each spread, pull the pop-up forwards and close the book carefully.

How to make a door

Use a craft knife to cut a door opening on pop-ups used as buildings, such as houses, shops or castles.

DESIGN TIPS

● Don't make pop-ups too big, or the space for writing will be too small.
● If the text is brief it will look better at the bottom of the page than at the top.
● Remind children to press pop-ups flat to draw on them.

4 · MORE POP-UP SHAPES

AGE
6–7

AIM: To make a simple pop-up story book with different shapes on each page.

PREPARATION: For each child, I made a pop-up book with a different pop-up on each of the three spreads.

🕐 Allow a 1-hour session for each of the three spreads.

How to use this project

Experiment with the basic pop-up technique (see pages 14–15) and see what new shapes you can come up with. Some children may be able to experiment with cutting different pop-up shapes on their own, using folded scrap paper.

Show children some different-shaped pop-ups and talk about what the shapes could represent. The children now look at the shapes in their own pop-up books. As a class, make a list of ideas for what the shapes could be. For example, the butterfly shape could also be a bow-tie or something exploding; the hexagon could be a jewel or the prow of a ship.

Using these lists, children make up a story based around the pop-up shapes, then write and draw it in their books.

DESIGN TIP

● Remember, pop-ups are made by cutting horizontally or diagonally across a fold. Be cautious if you find yourself cutting vertically. You might find that you are cutting the pop-up shape completely out of the paper!

How to make the book

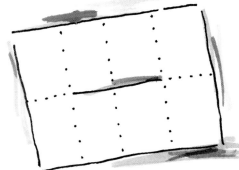

1 Use A3 paper to make an origami book to stage 3 (see page 7).

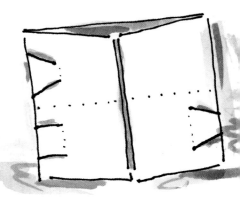

2 Fold the left and right edges to the centre. Cut and crease different shapes in three of the panels. A pop-up can be moved higher or lower on the page to provide a larger writing area.

3 Open out the paper and fold it into an origami book.

4

Lines starting
wide and
pointing
inwards
will make a
butterfly shape.

5

Parallel lines
will make a
box shape
(see page 14).
Lines starting
narrow and
pointing
outwards
will make
a hexagon.

Kaval (age 7) has
used his pop-up
shapes to tell the
story of a butterfly
that receives a
present with
a beautiful
ring inside.

MORE IDEAS

Pop-ins on Pop-outs!

Cut smaller
sections inside
the pop-outs
to pop-in!

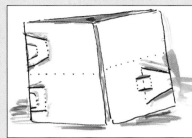

Experiment with how many different pop-ins on
pop-outs you can make on one single pop-up.

5 · POP-UP FACE BOOK

AIM: To create three characters and present them in a pop-up book of faces.

PREPARATION: I made a pop-up face book for each child, but children should be able to make the books alone.

 Allow a 1-hour session for each of the three spreads.

How to use this project

Share picture books with the class. What can the children tell about the characters from the illustrations? What can they tell about them from the text? Encourage children to use adjectives to describe the characters.

Children open their pop-up books to the first spread and draw a face on and around the nose. As they draw, discuss features such as earrings, hats and glasses. They write a description of the character on the left and right of the spread before starting on the next spread. Is something special happening to the character today, like a birthday treat, or a visit to a special friend?

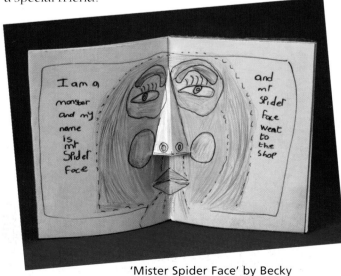

'Mister Spider Face' by Becky
(age 6)

How to make the book

1 Using A3 paper, make an origami book to stage 3 (see page 7).

2 Fold the left and right edges to the centre. Cut a 2 cm horizontal slit in the centre of three panels.

3 Fold a triangular flap up from the slit on the bottom panels and down on the top panel.

4 Unfold the flaps, then unfold the paper.

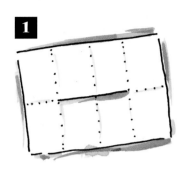

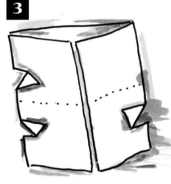

5 Fold into an origami book, making sure that the slit pages are inside.

6 Open each page and pull up the pop-up nose section.

A Family Portrait Album

On the first spread of the book, children draw a member of their generation (brother, sister or cousin); on the second, someone from their parents' generation (mother, father, uncle or aunt); on the third, someone from their grandparents' generation (grandfather or grandmother).

A Famous People Book

Children draw three of their favourite book characters, footballers or TV personalities. What can they find out about each one?

How to add a pop-up mouth

1

Make the face book to stage 4, then cut three extra, smaller slits as shown. Each of these will become a mouth.

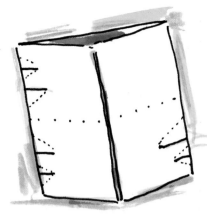

2

Fold a narrow triangle above and beneath each mouth slit. Unfold the paper and fold into an origami book as before.

3

Open each page and pull up the pop-up nose and mouth sections.

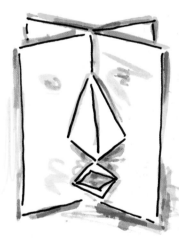

DESIGN TIPS

- For a larger nose, make a deeper cut.
- For a longer nose, extend the crease.

6 · POP-UP BUTTERFLY CARD

AGE
6-7

How to use this project

Use this project as preparation for making the butterfly story book (page 21). Show children pictures of real butterflies and discuss the variety of colour and pattern on the wings. I used *Wings – A Pop-up Book of Flight* by Nick Bantock (Bodley Head). Encourage children to notice the different parts to a butterfly's body, the number of legs, wings and antennae and to see where the wings attach.

For the wings, children choose a limited range of coloured pencils, such as red, blue and yellow and explore mixing them to produce secondary and tertiary colours. When they finish the wings, show children how to glue them to the base. They then imagine the butterfly's character, its name and where it lives, and write a caption on the card.

Christopher (age 6) had to think hard to find an appropriate caption.

How to make the card

1

Fold a sheet of A4 paper in half widthways.

2

Fold a 2 cm margin along the spine.

3

Open out the sheet and push the central crease upwards in the centre to form an inverted 'V'.

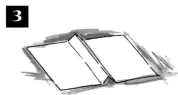
4

Cut an A4 sheet in half widthways. Cut a 2 cm margin from one long edge of each piece.

5

On the two sheets, draw and cut out these shapes. These will be the wings, with flaps to attach them.

6

Glue the flap on the left wing to the right side of the pop-up margin in the card.

7

Glue the other wing to the other side of the margin, so the wings interlock.

8

Move the edges of the finished card to make the butterfly fly.

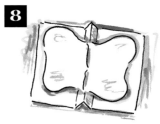

7 · BUTTERFLY BOOK

AGE 6-7

AIM: To make an origami book in the shape of a butterfly.

PREPARATION: I cut and folded a butterfly book for each child.

Allow three 1-hour sessions.

How to use this project

Talk about the differences between fiction and information books and ask pairs of children to sort some books into two sets, 'fiction' and 'information'. As a class, make up a story using children's butterfly cards as inspiration. Alternatively brainstorm ideas for an information book, using facts children have discovered from books about butterflies.

Before attempting the first spread of a butterfly story, the class think about what the butterfly is doing at the start of the narrative. On spread 2, they decide what the butterfly is going to do next. On the final spread, they think of a surprising end to the story. Brainstorm several different endings, then leave the children to choose their favourite one to use in their own books.

How to make the book

1

Use A4 paper to make an origami book to stage 2 (see page 7) but cut a triangle instead of a slit, as shown here. Cut the triangle narrow at the fold and wider at the crease.

2

Open out the paper, then fold it in half lengthways. Fold the tops of the left and right panels down to make triangular shapes.

3

Push the triangular shapes inside the horizontal fold.

4

Fold into an origami book. The finished book should resemble a butterfly.

How to make the book even more dynamic!

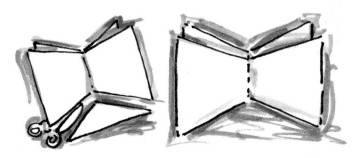

To make your book look even more like a butterfly, open the book to the centre and cut a wedge-shape through all the pages, from the bottom left and right corners.

8 · DAY-AND-NIGHT BOOK

AGE
6–7

> **AIM: To create a story book with a revolving disc that changes a scene from day to night.**
>
> **PREPARATION:** I cut and folded the pieces to make a day-and-night book for each child. Each child attached their disc when complete, with some help from me.
>
> Allow three 1-hour sessions.

How to use this project

Show children how the disc in their books can be turned to change the scene from day to night. Discuss things that can be only seen in the daytime, such as sunshine, open flowers and butterflies, and things that can only be seen at night, such as the moon, closed flowers and owls.

As a class, improvise a story about children playing inside the house during the day. Children draw the characters playing in the panel beneath the semicircle. On half of the disc, they draw a window showing the daytime sky, and on the other half, they draw a window with the night sky. When the disc is fastened into the book, children describe what the characters did during the day and in the evening.

'The Rainbow' by Leo (age 6). When the disc is turned, the rainbow disappears and a wild thunderstorm appears.

How to make the book

1

Fold an A3 sheet in quarters and unfold. In the top half of the bottom right panel cut a semicircular opening, leaving a small semicircle on the flat edge intact, as shown. Cut a smaller semicircle on the edge.

2

Cut a circle of thin card smaller than the width of the panel but larger than the semi-circle. Make a hole in the centre. Draw a line to divide it in half.

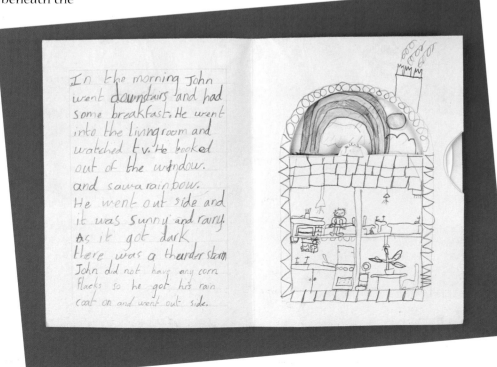

3

Fold the paper in half widthways and trace through the outline of the semicircular opening. Open out the paper and use a split pin to attach the disc in position on the back panel.

4

Fold the paper to greetings card form. To revolve the disc, turn the piece of card showing through the cut section at the edge.

MORE IDEAS

Favourite Toys

You can create four variations on the picture theme by cutting out a quarter circle section and dividing the disc into four. Can the children think of ideas for the book? How about a story with four episodes, or a book about animals or the seasons?

How to make a day-and-night flap book

1

Fold an A3 sheet into four and unfold. Cut the bottom right panel into two panels, as shown.

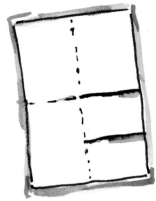

2

Fold the top half of the sheet behind the bottom half. Glue the lower right flap to the back sheet.

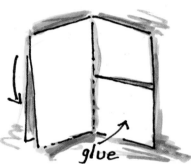

Children draw a party table with children eating and having fun in the bottom right panel. On the top flap, they draw a daytime sky scene and on the panel underneath, they draw a night sky scene. The left page is for writing all about the party, such as what was eaten and what games were played. Remember to write about the events during the day and the different things that happened when it got dark.

Lift the flap to change the scene from day to night.

9 · STAND-UP POP-UPS

AIM: To create a story in a concertina book with pop-ups that you can unfold.

PREPARATION: I made a four-page concertina pop-up book for each child and several spares for those who needed extra pages.

🕐 Allow about two hours.

How to use this project

As a class, read a story which contains a 'special' item: something with magic properties or an inanimate object that comes to life. Then use two objects as a starting point for an improvised story. I used a china cat and a paper dragon. Ask questions such as 'What happened the next day?' to prompt children to think about developing the story. They could then write their own story or rewrite the class story. If you decide to rewrite the class story, each group could be responsible for one part of it. The parts could then be joined together and displayed as a frieze.

How to make the book

1

Cut A3 paper in half lengthways.

2

Fold over a 1 cm margin on the right edge of one sheet.

3

Fold the left edge to the margin and unfold.

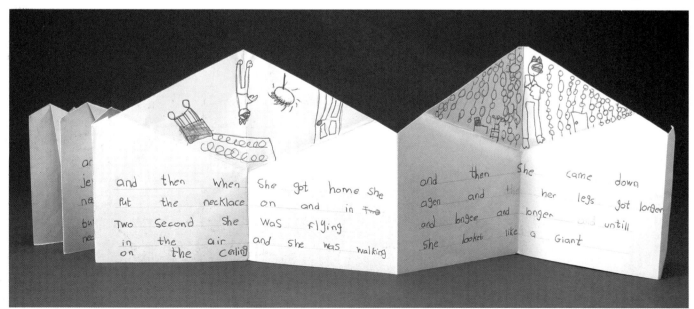

Sarah (age 6) uses the pop-ups to great effect in her magical story 'The Cat and the Dragon'.

4

Fold the left edge and the margin fold into the centre crease.

5

Cut out a shallow 'V' from the edges to the centre.

6

Fold the left and right panels down at a slight angle, then unfold.

7

Tuck the left and right top panels inwards on the creases.

8

Open out the paper and fold the centre crease forward to make a concertina. Repeat steps 2 to 7 with the second sheet. Glue the margin of the first sheet to the second sheet.

How to make figure pop-ups

It's simple to create a figure such as a giant, a king or a queen. Try animal shapes or buildings, too.

1

Make the stand-up pop-up book to stage 6.

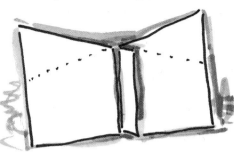

2

Draw half of a shape at the folded edge of each top panel. Cut around it. The shapes here will be a person and a house.

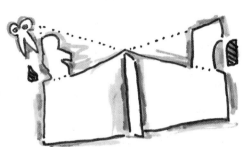

3

Cut away the triangular shape between the pop-ups so that the top is straight.

4

Continue as before.

DESIGN TIPS

● Make knife-sharp creases by running a fingernail along the folds.
● For this book to be most effective, display it with the base creased at a slight angle.

10 · CAROUSEL BOOK

AGE 6-7

How to use this project

Show children some books where the pictures give more information than the words alone, then talk about the way information can be conveyed in pictures as well as words. Brainstorm themes to go inside the four openings of the carousel book, such as the four seasons; morning, afternoon, evening and night; four contrasting shop windows, or a religious or folklore story. Children could make annotated drawings to plan their books, writing in note form rather than complete sentences. They draw on the four back panels and write the text or captions on the front panels before joining them together.

How to make the book

1

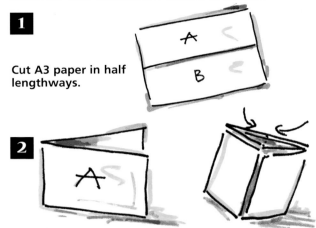

Cut A3 paper in half lengthways.

2

Fold the short ends of strip A together and unfold. Fold the left and right edges to the centre, then fold again to bring the new edges to the centre.

3

Open the whole sheet and concertina it along the creases.

4

Cut off a quarter of the length of strip B.

Once a cat called Sidney dreamed of living in a lovely HOUSE

Sidney also dreamed of making beautiful CLOTHES...

One night Sidney decided that it was silly to go on dreaming

Instead, he got his motor bike out and went on a real adventure.

Mariana (age 7) has given each opening a different shape and decoration.

26

5

Fold 1 cm margins at each end of strip B. Taking the margins as the ends, fold as for strip A (stage 2).

6

Open out strip B and concertina it along the creases.

7

Cut window openings on the folded edges of strip B opposite the margin edges.

8

Apply glue to the margins of strip B and to the back of the creases each side of the window panels. Fold the margins around the ends of strip A and press the glued creases to the creases on strip A.

How to add more layers

To make a more elaborate theatre, insert another layer between the front and back of the theatre.

Cut off one eighth of the length of the centre strip before folding and cutting as for stages 5 to 7.

MORE IDEAS

A Hanging Display

Attach the ends of the book together, tape on a length of cotton and hang it from the ceiling as a lantern. If possible, hang children's work at different lengths and in clusters.

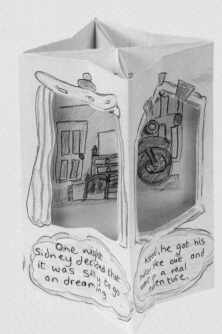

Change the Shape!

Cut angles at the top of the panels to make pointed archways and decorative finials.

DESIGN TIP

● Use small paperclips to hold the book in position when opened to a carousel shape.

11 · POP-UP THEATRE BOOK

AIM: To create three pop-up theatre scenes in a book.

PREPARATION: I made a pop-up theatre book for each child.

Allow a 1-hour session for each of the three spreads.

How to use this project

Share a story with the class, then help the children convert it into a play. Discuss what pictures children would need to draw in each of the three scenes of the theatre to make the background or 'set' for the story. What characters will they need to draw and cut out? Can the children work out what each character might say? Have children write down just each character's name followed by the words he or she should say.

'The Queen and the Treasure Chest' by Sarah (age 6) starts with the heroine centre stage with her treasure...

How to make the book

1 Use A3 paper to make an origami book to stage 2 (see page 7), but extend the slit beyond the centre crease to halfway across the next panel.

2 Fold the left and right edges to the centre. Cut widely spaced parallel slits in three of the sections, as shown.

3 Fold the slit sections forwards.

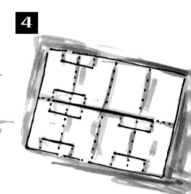

4 Unfold the sheet. (It will look like this.) Now fold into an origami book with the pop-up sections inside.

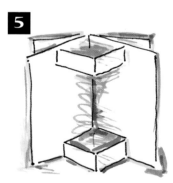

5 Open each spread and pull out the top and bottom sections. These make the stage. Scenery can now be drawn in between.

6 Characters are drawn on separate pieces of paper and then cut out. These can be glued onto the bottom pop-up section in each scene.

How to make a pop-up theatre card

A simplified pop-up theatre makes a quirky greetings card. Children should be able to fold this themselves, but they will need help with the cutting.

1 Fold a sheet of A4 paper in quarters and unfold.

2 Fold the paper lengthways, then cut halfway through the middle crease.

3 Fold the cut section towards you, then unfold.

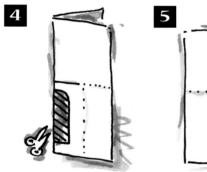

4 Cut out an arch-shape from the folded edge of the bottom half.

5 Open the sheet and fold the top half behind the bottom half.

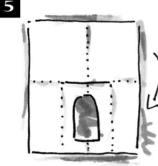

6 Fold the left edge to the right, pulling the pop-out section forwards.

7 Use the cut-out paper to draw characters. Glue them to the theatre.

MORE IDEAS

Mother's Day Card

Use the pop-up theatre card to make an unusual Mother's Day card. Each child draws a portrait of his or her mother in the theatre space and then decorates the edge of the theatre. What words are suitable for this card? What other occasions could it be used for?

Pop-up History

The pop-up theatre book makes a stunning way to present a history project. After researching life in Roman times, for example, they could choose three scenes to draw, such as the bath-house, a dinner party and the games.

DESIGN TIPS

● When children are folding paper and cutting with scissors, remember to give instructions appropriate for left-handed children.
● Flatten the pop-up stage to decorate it and to draw the backdrop.

and that Nate a robber came to steal The treasure chest and They left one coin on the froe and they dint see It on The froe

...but then a dastardly robber comes to the castle to steal the Queen's jewels.

29

12 · ANIMALS IN THE FRAME

AIM: To write and illustrate a story in a four-page book with a framed cover.

PREPARATION: I folded and cut a book for each child up to stage 2, then the children folded the book.

 Allow three 1½-hour sessions.

How to use this project

Talk about common themes in stories, such as the success of apparently weak characters, overcoming difficulties or searching for things or places. As a class, think up an animal character and improvise a four-part plot about such a theme. In part one, the character and setting are introduced. In part two, the character goes on an adventure. In part three, something exciting or frightening happens. Finally, in part four, the plot is resolved. Children then imagine their own animal character and give it a name and a personality. They illustrate the character in the book's framed cover, then work out the plot and write and illustrate the story.

How to make the book

1

Use A3 paper to make an origami book to stage 3 (see page 7). Cut down the top central fold.

2

In the bottom right panel, cut a door with a 2 cm margin around the edges. In the bottom left panel, cut a slot the same height as the door, 1 cm from the fold.

3

Fold the top panels behind the bottom panels.

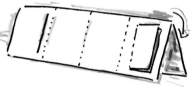

4

Push the middle panels together.

5

Fold the door and slot panels round the middle panels to form front and back covers.

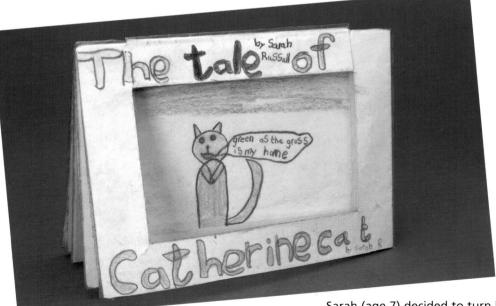

Sarah (age 7) decided to turn her book round so that the spine is at the top.

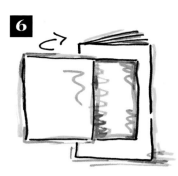

6

Open the door...

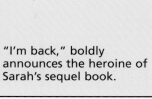

7

...and fold it around the back of the book, finally tucking it through the rear slot to make a spine.

How to make a book with 16 pages

Make two books to stage 6, cutting a door but no slot in one book, and a slot but no door in the other.

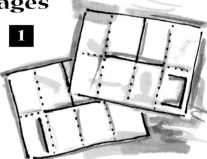

1

2

Insert the door through the slot on the back page of the other book. Put a spot of glue between the back of the first section and the front page of the second section to make sure they are joined together.

DESIGN TIPS

● Lightly glue down the outer cover panel so that it doesn't tear.
● Glue the door spine into the slot to stop it coming out when the book is opened.

MORE IDEAS

Book Sequel

Prompt children to extend their stories by asking a question such as 'What exciting thing happened the day after the story ended?' If ideas are slow to come, make a suggestion. Children could then write a sequel to the first book and weave a new adventure for their character.

"I'm back," boldly announces the heroine of Sarah's sequel book.

Inside, Catherine Cat's new adventure starts when she goes to the park.

13 · 'WHAT NEXT?' BOOK

AGE 7-8

AIM: To continue a story in a book that has a prescribed page layout.

PREPARATION: I made two A4 master sheets with different formats and duplicated two of each type per child. I made extras for drafting and additional pages. The children folded and stapled their sheets.

 Allow four 1½-hour sessions.

How to use this project

Read to your class a favourite book which has well-rounded characters and a lively plot. I used *The Giraffe and the Pelly and Me* by Roald Dahl (Puffin). To help children recognise how story characters are created, select words from the story and ask which characters they refer to. How can they tell? Discuss the main climax of the plot. How has the end of the story been made interesting? Ask the children to consider how they would like the story to continue and to write a one-sentence summary of this. They could share their ideas and vote for their favourite.

Children then continue the story from where it ends, using as many sheets as they need to write and illustrate it. Each frame must contain an illustration and the text must fit in the space around it.

How to make the sheets

1

Fold an A4 sheet widthways and draw an illustration frame with a generous margin on the right side of the page.

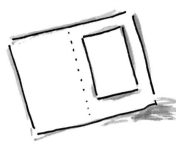

2

On another folded sheet, draw one illustration frame bottom left and one top right.

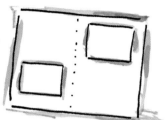

3

Duplicate sheets and fold in half with the blank side inside.

Text and pictures work together to tell the story 'Billy meets his Friends' by Mariana (age 8). When designing these pages, I included dotted lines to guide the children's handwriting.

Colour Coding

Photocopy the master sheets onto different coloured paper to make a book with colour-coded sections. For example, green pages could be for the introduction (all about our visit to a museum), yellow pages could be for information (describing the main exhibition), blue pages could be for further information (other things on display) and red pages for comment (what I enjoyed most).

Class Chapter Story

You could use this technique to write a class story. One child starts the story off with chapter one, writing and drawing on both sheets of paper. The next child reads the story so far and adds chapter two. Continue around the class in this way until the final child finishes off the story.

The front cover introduces the reader to all Billy's friends.

DESIGN TIPS

● Use coloured paper for the cover.
● Make sure that children write on the pages the right way up and that they don't write too near the edges or the centre fold.

How to make the cover

Children should be able to fold and attach this cover themselves with some guidance.

1 Fold A3 paper in half widthways. Open it out and lay a sheet of A4 paper in the centre, as shown.

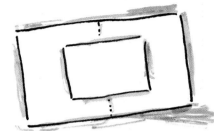

2 Fold the top and bottom edges along the edges of the A4 sheet.

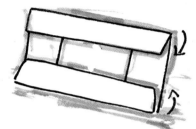

3 Fold the left and right edges over the A4 sheet. Remove the A4 paper and fold along the creases again.

4 Put the book pages in order and add a plain folded sheet to each end. Staple through the open edges of the pages.

5 Tuck the first and last pages into the the left and right pockets of the cover.

14 · PAGE-AT-A-TIME BOOK

AIM: To write a story on separate pieces of paper which are then joined to make a book.

PREPARATION: Each child made a concertina base and I provided four pages to go inside each base.

 Allow four 2-hour sessions.

How to use this project

Introduce the class to an exciting picture book about the adventures of one character. I used Brian Wildsmith's *Bear's Adventure* (Oxford University Press). Introduce the word 'episode', and ask children what the main episodes in the story were. Children then rewrite the story in their own words, adding new material or changing the story. Assess the merits of each page of writing or illustration with children as they are completed. Some rewriting or more drawing may be necessary before the pages are glued into the concertina base.

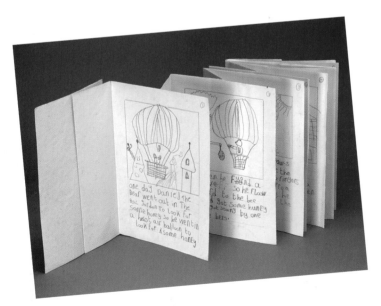

In this extended page-at-a-time book by Oliver (age 7), Bear rides on a balloon, then on a dragon and has a great deal to eat along the way!

How to make the book

1

Cut A3 paper in half lengthways.

2

Crease one piece of paper into eight concertina folds (see stages 2 to 3 on page 26).

3

Fold the second strip into quarters and cut to make four panels.

4

When the story is complete, glue the left edge of each panel to the right side of each spread on the concertina base.

MORE IDEAS

Class Contribution Book

Every child contributes a prayer, poem, riddle or any other short text to the book. This is an ideal occasion for developing fine handwriting skills or computer word-processing. Explore ways of decorating the panels. Can the letter shapes themselves be incorporated into the design?

15 · INVITATION CARD

AGE
8-9

AIM: To design an invitation to the launch of a new book.

PREPARATION: Each child folded their own invitation card and cut the flap with some assistance from me.

 Allow two 1-hour sessions.

How to use this project

Show children examples of publishing logos, and encourage them to think up their own, such as 'Sunshine Books' or 'Beaver Road Publishing plc'. Talk about the role of publishers, explaining that while authors write books, publishers are responsible for producing copies of the books and for selling them. Children then make an invitation to a book launch. They design a simple cover with attractive patterns surrounding a few words such as 'Please open' or 'An invitation'. On the inside left is a picture of the book's cover. They write details of the invitation under the flap and on the reverse side of the flap, write 'RSVP'.

Sarah's invitation to the launch of her own book, 'Catherine Cat Again'.

How to make the card

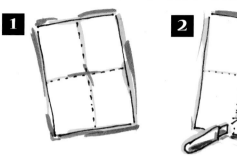

1 Fold A4 paper in half and half again. Unfold the paper.

2 Cut a flap in the bottom right quarter as shown.

3 Fold the paper again and crease back the flap.

MORE IDEAS

A Promotional Book Flyer

Children fold A4 paper in half to make a leaflet. On the front, they draw the book's cover, a catchy sentence, such as 'A thrilling new book from the author of...' and a publisher's logo. Discuss what a buyer wants to know about the book. The children write this information on the inside left page. They make the inside right page into an order form, and write the address on the back so that the form can be cut out and sent off.

16 · POETRY FOLDER

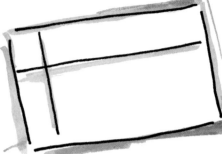

AGE 8–9

AIM: **To make a class collection of poems and drawings, and present them in a folder.**

PREPARATION: I made the folder for all the children's work.

🕐 Allow half a morning for a class visit and two 1½-hour sessions for writing and drawing.

How to use this project

Children visit a park, garden or woodland and collect, sketch and make notes about what catches their eye. Ask them to think about ways to describe an object, using as few words as possible to say how it feels, smells or looks. Does it remind them of something else? Back in the classroom, children make a list of important words, then write down other words which go with them. They use their work to write a short poem. Children draw a 1 cm margin around a sheet of A4 paper and with the paper arranged landscape, lay out the poem with a drawing of the object. The finished sheets are collated in the folder.

How to make the folder

1

Using A2 cartridge paper or thin card, draw a line 13 cm from the left edge and another 9 cm from the top edge.

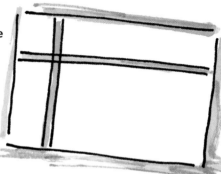

2

Draw a 1 cm-wide margin to the right of the first line and below the second.

3

Turn the paper round and repeat.

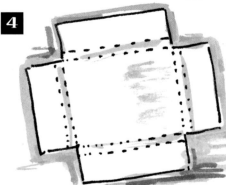

4

Cut out the corner panels.

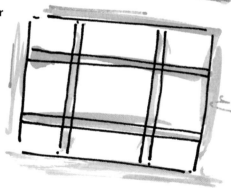

This poetry folder contains another, smaller folder inside, with the sides cut down. The inner folder frames the work inside.

5

Slightly taper the edges of the flaps. Use a ruler and a craft knife to gently score all the lines.

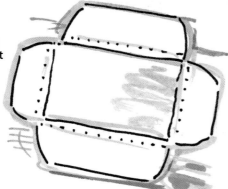

6

Fold as shown.

7

Interlock the cover flaps to complete the folder.

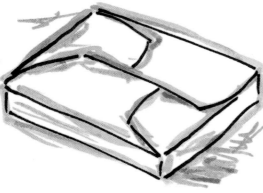

How to make a mount

This raised mount can be used to display work from the poetry folder.

1

Use a craft knife to cut cartridge paper slightly larger than A4, as shown.

2

Fold the central panels so that the edges touch the outer edges of the frame.

3

Fold in the edges of the two panels to the edge of the window.

4

Glue the bottom edges of the folded panels to a base.

5

Display the work inside the window.

MORE IDEAS

Class Display

The advantage of removable pages is that they can be mounted as a wall display or passed around the class so that every child can examine one.

DESIGN TIP

● Use quality paper, perhaps tinted or textured, to encourage children to produce quality work.

17 · HOLIDAY BROCHURE

AGE 8–9

AIM: To design, write and illustrate a holiday brochure.

PREPARATION: I cut and folded one brochure for each group of six children. They shared the making of the brochure between them.

Allow two 2-hour sessions.

How to use this project

Children look at holiday brochures, and make a list of the essential features included on them, such as addresses and lists of facilities. Working in groups of six, they then design and create their own brochure. Encourage children to draft material, share ideas and discuss each other's copy.

How to make the brochure

1

Fold A2 paper widthways into three equal panels and unfold. Then fold the paper in half lengthways and unfold.

2

Cut down the top left crease and the bottom right crease, as shown.

3

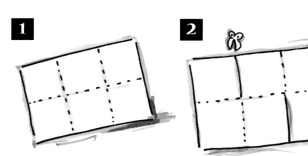

Cut out a window on the right of the top left panel and cut a hinged door on the top right panel.

4

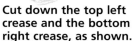

Swing panels A around on the middle crease.

5

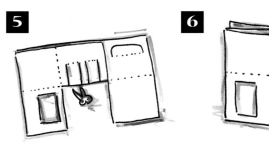

Cut four parallel slits through the middle fold halfway into the panels.

6

Fold the two left panels in front of the middle panel and the two right panels behind.

7

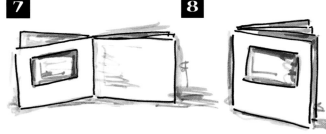

Turn the book around so that the right edge now becomes the bottom of the book.

8

Fold the window panel to the right. Fold the remaining left panel behind the book.

One child designs an eye-catching cover for the group brochure. Another child traces through the cover frame onto paper slightly smaller than page size. A picture is drawn in the panel and text added around it. When complete, this is glued onto page 3.

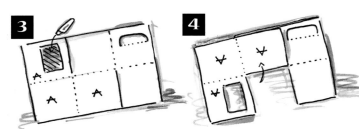

A third child writes special offers for customers on spare paper. The copy is glued to pages 4 and 5, and the pop-ups are designed to match.

A fourth child describes the hotel facilities, then glues them to page 6 and designs the movable hotel-room door.

On the opposite page, a fifth child prepares a list of things to take on holiday, such as a first-aid kit, foreign currency and clothes.

Meanwhile, a sixth child lays out a booking form to be glued on the back cover.

MORE IDEAS

Advertising and Information

This brochure format can be applied to all sorts of advertising or information brochures, such as for a stately home, a garden centre, a football club or recycling in the home.

Travel Agent

Children who finish their task ahead of the others could design other things a travel agent might provide, such as a luggage label, holiday poster, a discount coupon or a document wallet.

Encourage children to use eye-catching lettering and colours for posters.

18 · PORTRAIT BOOK

AGE 8–9

AIM: To make a class book of portraits to which each child contributes a drawing and text.

PREPARATION: I provided strips of paper which the children creased into sections for the concertina book. I made a cover and helped attach the pages.

 Allow two 2-hour sessions.

How to use this project

Arrange the children around tables with plants or ornaments in the centre. Supply paper that is 4 cm smaller on all sides than the final page. Children draw the still-life in the bottom half of the paper. They use the person opposite them as inspiration to draw a portrait in the top half, with an imaginary background. On a piece of same size paper, children write a description to accompany the picture.

Children glue their artwork onto a slightly larger piece of coloured paper. The artwork and text are then pasted into the concertina book.

How to make the book

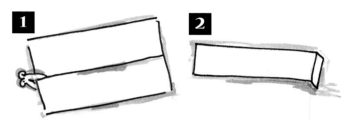

1 Cut an A2 sheet of paper in half lengthways.

2 Fold a 1 cm margin on the right edge of one sheet.

3 Fold the left edge to the margin fold. Open out and fold the left edge and the right margin to the centre crease. Fold into a concertina.

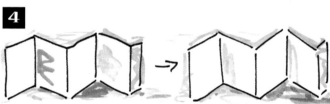

4

Repeat with the second sheet, then join the right margin of the first sheet to the rear side of the left edge of the second sheet. Repeat until there is a spread for each child.

Each child introduces the next character by ending their piece of writing with the words "This person has a friend called..."

How to make the cover

1

Cut two pieces of thick card slightly larger than one concertina page. Cut a card strip 4 cm wide for the spine.

2

Glue the pieces lightly down onto A3 paper as shown. Allow a 2 cm border at the edges. Trim away any surplus paper.

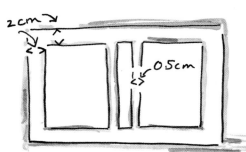

3

Cut diagonally across the corners, as shown.

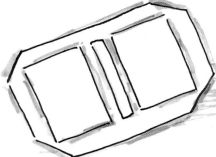

4

Apply glue to the paper borders and fold them over the card.

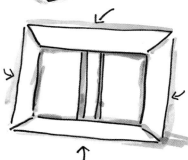

5

Cut a piece of copy paper to cover the spine and the edges of the card. Glue it on and crease it by folding the cover together.

6

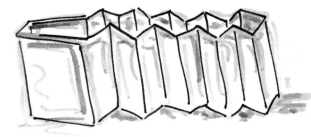

Glue the first page of the book to the inside front cover and the last page to the inside back cover.

MORE IDEAS

Class Project Book

With each child contributing one spread, all sorts of class books can be created. You could make an outline of a current history or geography project, such as 'All about the Romans' or 'Life in an African village'. Or use the book for a different creative writing and drawing project. As a class, choose a theme such as 'The most exciting day of my life', 'My most frightening experience' or 'What I would like to be doing in twenty years time' and ask children to write and draw pages on the theme.

All About Us

Children could draw a portrait of their 'sitter' and write a description of the person to go with the drawing. Children could 'interview' their partners to find out extra details about them, such as their likes and dislikes, their favourite sport or musical group, the names of their pets, and so on. Join all the children's work together to make a fascinating document about the class.

DESIGN TIPS

● Use minimal amounts of glue to join the pages and make the cover.
● When pressing down glued sections, lay a spare piece of paper over the area first. This prevents fingermarks showing.

19 · POP-UP SHIP BOOK

AIM: To make a pop-up ship book, combining technology, art and writing skills.

PREPARATION: Children did the cutting, folding and assembly of the ship by themselves. I made the book cover and attached all the spreads to make a class book.

 Allow four 2-hour sessions.

How to use this project

A project about ancient travel could stimulate this pop-up book about a sailing ship. Decide with the class whether the book will be historical, scientific or a story. Discuss the tense used for writing a descriptive report. Most verbs are in the present, though some may be in the past, referring to things which have been done or made. Children can make notes from reference books, videos or CD-ROMs for their research. Encourage them to use glossaries to find the meanings of 'ship' words. You could create a class ship vocabulary dictionary.

Allow children to make a trial ship using A4 copy paper, then use A3 cartridge paper to make the final piece (twice the size). Design the base artwork and write the text before joining the ship to it. Decorate the ship pieces before assembling them, drawing on both sides of pieces such as figures and sails.

How to make the book

1

Cut A4 copy paper in half widthways.

2

Fold one of the pieces in half widthways and unfold. This forms the base.

3

Cut the other piece in half lengthways. For one strip, fold a small margin on the right edge.

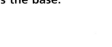

'The Ferrit' by Gemma (age 9) is one of many beautiful pop-up ships that were glued into a class book.

4

Glue the left edge of the strip to the margin and flatten the loop.

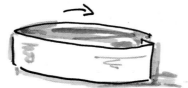

5

Cut the bottom edge of the flattened loop as shown (cut through both sides). This gives you a central tab on each side.

6

Apply glue to the outside of each tab. Lay the shape on one side of the base with the tab close to the centre crease. Close the base and press down.

7

Open out the base to raise the hull of the ship.

8

Cut a cabin, masts and sails from the remaining strip and glue into place inside the hull. Try to ensure that nothing sticks out when the base sheet is closed.

MORE IDEAS

All Sorts of Ships

Experiment with designing different kinds of craft, such as a fishing boat, a luxury cruiser or a sailing dinghy. Use reference books to help identify different hull shapes and rigging. As children become more competent at making pop-ups, new design challenges can be explored, such as a set of flags hanging from the rigging and cut-out figures glued on to the deck or in the crow's nest.

How to make a class book

An effective way of presenting the work is to bind a group of pop-ups into one hard-covered book (see page 41 for details on how to make the cover). To join the pop-up pages, glue the back of the right page to the back of the next left page.

DESIGN TIPS

● For the finished piece, glue the pop-ups to the flat ship and not in the standing position.
● Keep the depth of the hull quite shallow so that there is a large area for the cabin and sails above it.

20 · POP-UP SHIP LEAFLET

AIM: To make a pop-up leaflet to promote the class book of ships.

PREPARATION: Children folded, cut and engineered the pop-up to stage 4. I provided the strips of paper for the mast and sail.

 Allow a 1-hour session for making the leaflet and 1½ hours for the artwork and text.

How to use the project

Discuss the ways that promotional writing entices the reader to enquire further. Brainstorm captions, trying to avoid over-used ones. Give children a word limit of perhaps ten words, and ask them to draft three lines of promotional copy for the pop-up ship book they made on pages 42 and 43 before choosing one for the leaflet.

Children first practise making the pop-up using A4 copy paper, then repeat using A3 cartridge paper. Text and artwork are added before assembling the leaflet. The cover is designed last of all.

Alex (age 9) has kept the message simple in his leaflet.

How to make the leaflet

1 Fold the paper in quarters, then unfold.

2 Fold the paper in half lengthways. Cut a curve on the bottom fold.

3 Fold the curved shape at an angle, then unfold.

4 Open the leaflet. Fold the top half behind the bottom half. Pull out the pop-up. Fold to make a card.

5 Cut a piece of paper to make the sail and fold in half.

6 Cut a strip of paper half as tall as the leaflet. Fold it in half and cut a short slit along the fold. Fold up the two flaps.

7 Dab glue on the flaps and press them inside the pop-up so that the mast stands straight. Glue the sail to the mast.

DESIGN TIPS

● When folding down the pop-up hull shape, make sure that it does not stick over the edge of the page.
● If the sail is too large, the weight of it may bend the mast.

21 · LIFT-THE-FLAP LEAFLET

> **AIM:** To create a lift-the flap leaflet for a charity organisation.
>
> **PREPARATION:** I cut and folded a leaflet for each child.
>
> Allow one 2-hour session.

How to use this project

Ask children to consider the headlines used in charity leaflets and advertisements. Discuss the ways charities appeal to people by trying to make them feel guilty, concerned or hopeful.

Discuss what will go on the front cover of the children's own leaflets. Inside, the left flap is for a rich child's suitcase; the right flap is for a poor child's suitcase. Imagine how different the contents of the two suitcases will be. In the bottom half of the page, the text tells people why and how to donate to the charity. In pairs or groups, children make notes of the information they want to provide to persuade people to give money, and then brainstorm phrases which will present the information as briefly as possible.

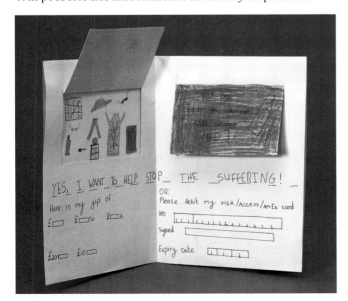

For extra effect, Eric (age 9) coloured in his illustration of a rich child's belongings but left the poor child's few possessions as pencil outlines.

How to make the leaflet

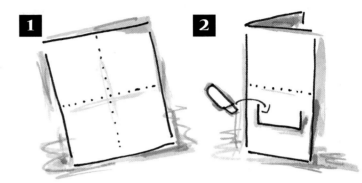

1 Fold A3 copy paper into quarters and unfold.

2 Now fold in half and cut a flap through the top of both bottom panels, as shown.

3 Unfold the paper. Fold the top half behind the bottom half. Fold into a card.

MORE IDEAS

Hidden Surprises

This lift-the-flap technique can be used to make a riddle and answer challenge or a before-and-after leaflet, perhaps for an ecological project showing the effects of pollution on a landscape. With a sideways-opening door, it could be a welcome to an adventure playground, a seaside attraction or a birthday party.

DESIGN TIP

● Working in small groups, children can practise cutting the flaps with a craft knife.

22 · DIARY

AGE 9–10

AIM: To write an imaginary diary in a book with its own paper lock.

PREPARATION: I creased and cut the paper, but children assembled the book. I cut the paper locks and the slots, then the children threaded the strip to make the lock.

 Allow four 2-hour sessions.

How to use this project

Describe what writing in the first person means, then choose a familiar story and discuss the changes needed to make it into a diary of the main character. Children then write a diary from the point of view of someone else. It could be an animal or even an inanimate object. To get children thinking of things to put in the diary, they could make lists of things people do, things that can go wrong or unexpected people who can turn up. They can look through their lists to create a plot for the diary.

The first page of the book is for the title, then there is a spread each for Monday to Saturday. The last, single page is for Sunday. Each left page could be divided into sections for morning, afternoon and evening or night. The right page is used for illustration.

How to make the book

1

Fold A2 paper in half widthways. Open out and fold left and right edges to the centre. Unfold the sheet, turn it around and repeat the folding lengthways.

2

You now have 16 small panels. With the paper in landscape position, make three cuts across three panels as shown.

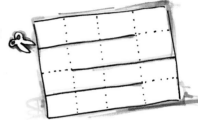

3

Starting from the top left corner, fold each panel in a zig-zag, continuing the pattern when you come to a corner.

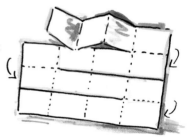

4

This will make a 16-page book.

A single paper-strip creates the spine and lock for 'Lizzy's Daring Diary' by Mariana and Elizabeth (age 9).

5

Cut a strip of paper from the short side of an A2 sheet.

6

Bend the first and last pages away from the rest of the pages and lay them on the table next to each other. Cut two slots slightly larger than the width of the strip through both pages.

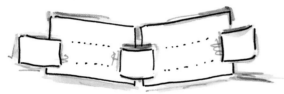

7

Thread the strip through the slots to make a spine.

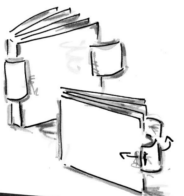

8

Close the book. Tuck the ends of the strip through the slots to lock the book.

How to change the locks

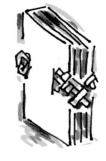

Experiment with using decorative ribbon in place of paper. Tie a bow to 'lock' the book closed.

For another decorative lock, plait two strips of paper as a locking strip.

MORE IDEAS

Personal Diary

Instead of using a fictional character, children could keep a daily journal. What were the high points and low points of each day? They could write about their hobbies or interests, or about their favourite school subjects.

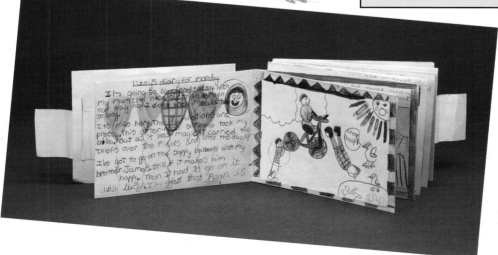

In 'Lizzy's Daring Diary', robbers steal the heroine's magic bike but come to a sticky end before the week is out.

23 · SUITCASE BOOK

AGE 9–10

 AIM: To write a holiday adventure story in a suitcase-shaped book.

PREPARATION: The children made the concertina pages but I cut and folded the covers for each book.

Allow three 2-hour sessions.

How to use this project

Tell the class that they are going to write a story about a holiday where everything goes wrong! Talk about what could happen and where. Consider the preparations, the journey, the arrival, and so on. Discuss what makes a good plot (such as climaxes and resolutions) and how to make characters sound real. Children start with an enticing first sentence, then plan at least two calamities for each page. The book can extend to any number of pages. Write the book title on the first right page and start writing on the next page. The cover is designed to look like a suitcase with the author's name on the label.

'Bong Bong Pop Island' by Emma (age 9) begins with a dramatic plane crash!

How to make the book

1

Using A3 paper, make a concertina book as described on page 40.

2

Cut a strip of thin card slightly higher than the pages inside and 1 cm wider on each side.

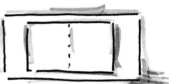

3

Fold the left edge to 1 cm from the right edge and unfold. Fold the right edge to 1 cm from the left edge and unfold.

4

Bend in both sides to make a cover with a spine.

5

Glue the first and last page of the book inside the covers.

6

Make two handles from thin card. Glue them to the inside edges of the front and back covers. Make a label and tie it to a handle with thread.

24 · TOYSHOP BOOK AGE 9-10

AIM: To create a concertina book for a story with detailed illustrations.

PREPARATION: I made the concertina page sections and the children made their own covers.

Allow four 2-hour sessions.

How to use this project

Tell the class the first few lines of a story, such as: 'Near where Adam lived was a toyshop. It sold some of the best toys in the world…' After discussing the possibilities, children continue the story. They create a storyboard for their story (see page 13), then begin to draw in their books. The idea is to gradually build up the detail in each illustration until it tells a story by itself. For example, they could sketch a row of shops, then add signs to each door, objects in each window, people in the upstairs windows and posters on the walls. Children now write words to the story, expanding on their brief storyboard sentences to paint a clearer picture. Add extra pages until the story is completed.

How to make the book

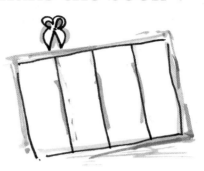

1

Cut A2 paper widthways into four equal strips.

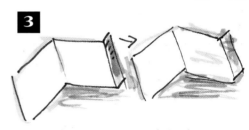

2

Fold a 1 cm margin on the right edge of each strip. Fold the left edge to the margin, crease, then unfold.

3

Glue the margin of the first sheet to the reverse left edge of the next sheet, and so on until all four sheets are joined.

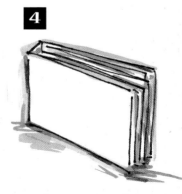

4

Make a cover as for stages 2 to 5 of the Suitcase Book (see page 48).

Lennard (age 10) has packed so much detail into his illustrations that the reader is constantly spotting new things.

25 · THROUGH-THE-DOOR BOOK

AGE 9–10

How to use this project

Read the extract in the opening of *The Hobbit* by JRR Tolkien (HarperCollins) which describes Bilbo Baggins' home, including the door. Tell children that they are going to design and describe doors and what lies behind them with the same level of detail. Show pictures of different doors and brainstorm ideas for rooms which could lie behind them. Can they tell what is behind a door just by looking at it? How would they describe the door?

Children write a description of a room on a piece of paper and fix it to the inside left page of their section. They decorate the door and surrounding area on the right page. On a separate piece of paper, slightly smaller than the page, children draw the room behind the door (this will be glued in place later.) The rest of the room is drawn on the reverse of the door page.

A bucket of water lurks above this door to douse unsuspecting entrants.

How to make the book

1 To make one section, cut A2 paper in half lengthways. Fold one of the strips in half widthways and unfold. Cut a central door in the right panel.

2 Glue each room scene to the front of another child's section. Cut and fold a strip of paper to glue each section to the next. Glue the last child's work onto a blank sheet.

Room scene

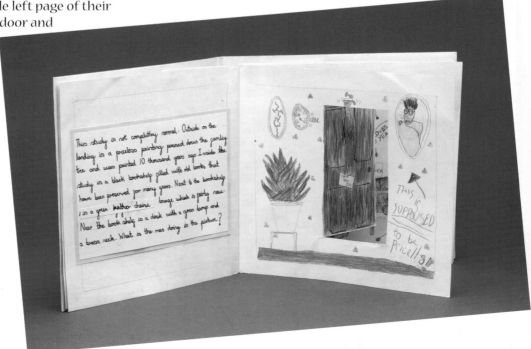

More Interesting Doors

Children could design all sorts of elaborate doors with decorative keyholes, opening letterboxes, door knockers or signs.

DESIGN TIP

● When cutting sections, line up the doors so that they are in the same position throughout the book.

Turn the page to discover this boy's dream bedroom, complete with drinks machine!

How to make a through-the-door concertina book

This book idea is perfect for creating an imaginary house. Children write a description of each room on the left page then draw it as seen through the open door. Add extra concertina sections as necessary.

1

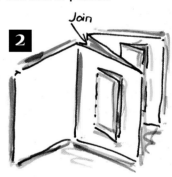

Concertina a strip of paper into four panels. Cut a door on the second and fourth panels.

2

Glue the back of the second page to the back of the third page.

3

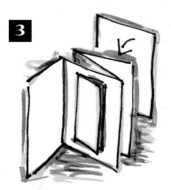

Glue a sheet of paper behind the fourth page, or if the book continues, glue it to the front page of the next concertina.

26 · HOBBY BOOK I

How to use this project

A week or two before the project, children decide what subject their book will be about and begin to research the subject or gather material from home, such as their own stamp collection or a selection of books about caring for rabbits.

Discuss devices used in information books to help the reader, such as boxes, bullet points, captions and different type sizes or styles. Look at the way books are arranged, with a contents page at the beginning and a glossary and index at the end. Children now plan their book, remembering to allow space for page headings, diagrams and drawings. Completed pages are arranged in order and checked (any pages which don't seem as good as the rest can be reworked.) After the text is complete, children can re-read it and list the words that should be in the glossary and index. They finally design the book cover, making it different from the title page design by rearranging the text and images.

The theme of this project is entirely child-led. Hobby Book II (see page 56) gives children a further opportunity to tackle their own subject matter and put into practice book-making skills that they have learned.

How to make the book cover

1 Fold A2 paper in half lengthways.

2 Then fold the paper in half widthways.

3 To make the spine, fold a 4 cm margin from the middle fold, as shown.

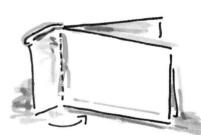

4 Fold the spine panel in half to touch the margin crease, then unfold.

5 Open out the spine and fold the creases in a zig-zag as shown.

How to make the pages

1

Remove 4 cm from one short edge of A4 paper. Repeat with all pages (or use a guillotine).

2

Slot the pages into the central fold of the spine.

3

Hold the pages in place using paperclips. These will be hidden by the covers.

Mariana (age 9) chose to make a book about the stamp collection she had just started.

MORE IDEAS

Page Plan

With a complex book like this, it is helpful to make a page plan at the start to organise the contents. Children write down the headings of chapters, and make page-by-page notes of what the text will say under each chapter heading. If subheadings, drawings, diagrams or charts are to be included, these should be noted in the appropriate place. When children write a first draft of text, they can check back to see that they have the right information in the right place.

DESIGN TIPS

● Every so often, children should lay their pages out in front of them and check consistency of handwriting and layout.
● Encourage children to achieve a balance between writing and illustration across their book.

27 · SPECIAL CONCERTINA BOOK

AIM: To combine a concertina book and a pop-up theatre.

PREPARATION: I made a theatre for each pair of children to stage 6, then they cut, folded and glued in the scenery panel and background artwork. Children folded and attached their own concertina books.

 Allow three 2-hour sessions.

How to use this project

As a class, read an article about an issue such as endangered species, genetically modified foods or pollution. Ask children to identify fact and opinion. If possible read another article on the same topic giving a different point of view. Can children explain the differences? Discuss agencies such as Greenpeace which try to help endangered animals and habitats.

In pairs, children improvise a story about people working for such an agency. Child 1 then designs the scenery, while child 2 draws the background. These pieces are glued into the theatre. To create the book, child 1 writes the first part while child 2 illustrates it, then they alternate roles for the rest of the book.

How to make the theatre

1

Cut A3 paper in half lengthways. Take one strip and fold a 1 cm margin on the right edge.

2

Fold the left edge to the right fold and unfold.

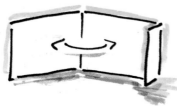

3

Fold the right creased edge in to make a 4 cm flap.

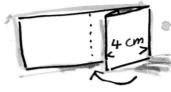

4

Fold the left edge to the flap. Unfold.

5

Cut a large window in the left panel.

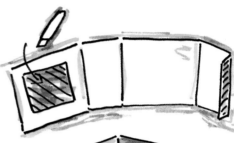

6

Glue the left edge to the right margin.

7

Cut a strip the same height as the theatre and 2 cm wider. Fold back 1 cm margins on each side. Cut a scenery outline from the centre panel.

8

Glue the scenery into the theatre. Cut a background panel to fit the back of the theatre and glue it in place.

How to make the book

1

Fold the leftover paper strip as for stages 1 and 2.

2

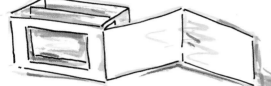

Glue the margin to the right side of the theatre.

3

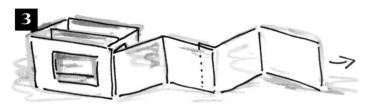

Make as many pages as required and use the margin for joining them together.

4

The theatre and pages will close down flat.

Amna and Sarah (age 10) have attached another flap of paper to the left of the theatre to make a title page for their book about saving animals.

MORE IDEAS

Simple Theatre

A simpler way to make the theatre is to leave out the scenery so that the viewer looks through the window to the artwork on the back panel.

DESIGN TIPS

● Cut away enough of the scenery to allow the backdrop of the theatre to be seen.
● Use contrasting colouring for the front of the theatre and the scenery so that both stand out.

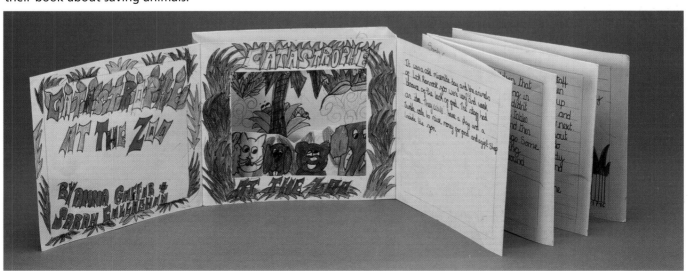

28 · HOBBY BOOK II

AIM: To plan the contents of a book about an interest or hobby, then write and illustrate it in a concertina book.

PREPARATION: I made the concertina page sections for each child's book. The children glued the sections together and made covers for their books.

 Allow four 2-hour sessions.

How to use this project

In this project, children research and collect resource material a week before the project begins. Then, they prepare page plans (see page 53), and discuss their plans with partners, asking questions like: 'Will someone like me want to read this book?', 'Have I put the parts of the book together in the best order?' and 'Can I produce enough material under each heading to fill the page?' They revise the plan, going into more detail and, when they are happy with it, write and draw the book itself.

Sarah (age 10) needed lots of extra pages to complete her 'ABC Guide to Keeping Cats'.

How to make the book

Make a concertina book and cover as for the Portrait Book (see page 40).

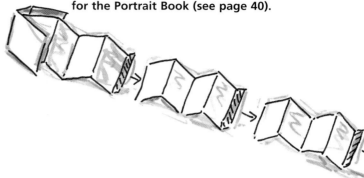

DESIGN TIP

● Vary the placing of illustrations on different pages throughout the book.

MORE IDEAS

Mixing Techniques

Sarah used a lift-the-flap technique to make a cat flap.

Children can use this book as an opportunity to combine different techniques they have learned. For example, box pop-ups (see page 14) could be cut into the folds, or the pages could be arch-shaped like the carousel book (see page 26).

29 · HOBBY BOOK FLYER

 AGE 10-11

 AIM: To produce a leaflet with a pop-up book inside, to advertise a real book made by the child.

PREPARATION: I folded and cut the flyer for each child up to stage 3. Children folded out the pop-up section.

Allow 2 hours.

How to use this project

Use a display of advertisements to discuss advertising with the class. Can children identify phrases designed to conjure up particular images? Can they find any similes? Discuss different ways to promote a book. What would make people read their book? What's the most exciting thing about it? What's interesting about the author? Children write and discuss their first drafts before transferring them to the flyer. On the outside, they design catchy artwork with no words. Inside, they press the pop-up flat and draw the cover of the promoted book. They use the remaining space to describe the book and its author.

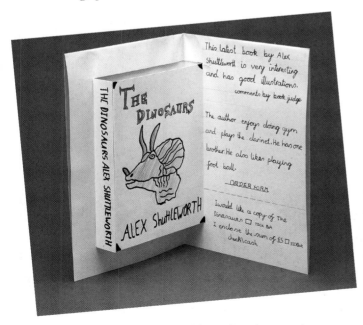

Don't forget to write the title and author on the 'spine' of the pop-up book, as Alex (age 10) has done.

How to make the flyer

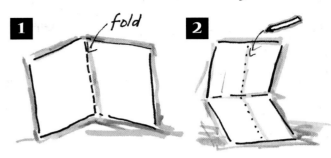

1 Fold A3 paper in half widthways and then unfold it.

2 Use a pencil and ruler to draw a line down the centre of the paper lengthways.

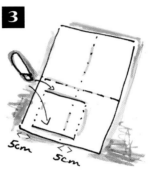 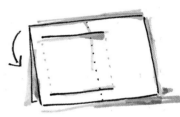

3 Cut two parallel lines in the bottom section, about 5 cm in from the left edge to 5 cm over the vertical line.

4 Fold the top half of the paper behind the bottom half.

5 Crease each side of the cut section against a ruler.

6 Close the book (smooth the cut section towards the open edge to fold it). Open out to see the pop-up book.

30 · WORLD WAR II BOOK

AIM: To create a four-part pop-up book on an historical theme.

PREPARATION: Each child made the basic book prior to the project in small groups so that I could help where required. I cut the basic pop-up shapes, and the children did the folding and gluing.

 Allow six 2-hour sessions.

How to use this project

This book tells the story of a family living in a terraced house in Britain during World War II. The text can be recorded information or a first person narrative from the point of view of a person living in the house. The children research the subject, using information books, fiction, poetry and personal accounts. Talk about what day-to-day life was like in wartime. What was it like to use an air-raid shelter? Can children imagine what it would feel like to have their home bombed? Write a list of wartime words and phrases such as 'blackout', 'Dig for Victory' and 'all-clear'. For each spread, children write the text and do the artwork before gluing the pop-ups in place.

How to make the book

1

Make an A2 origami book to stage 6 (see page 7). Glue the top and bottom edges of one of two panels that are open at the top and bottom.

2

Cut through the vertical crease of the other panel that is open at the top and bottom. This makes two single panels.

3 These two single panels become the front and back covers of the book.

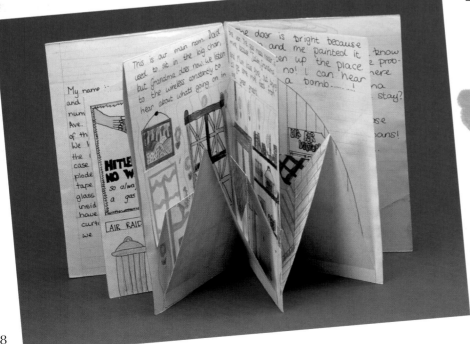

After some careful research, Liz (age 10) created a wartime house full of fascinating details.

How to make the house

The first spread shows the outside of a typical terraced house during World War II, with sticky tape on the windows and wartime posters on the walls.

1

Take a piece of A5 paper and remove 4 cm from one short edge.

2

Fold in half lengthways. Fold 1 cm margins along the two long edges, then unfold.

3

Fold the paper along the central crease Apply glue to the margins on the outside.

4

Align the central fold with the edge of the page and close the page.

5

The house pops up in the centre of the spread when opened.

Liz's text runs in two columns down each side of the house. It introduces the main character and explains details of the illustration, such as the taped windows and an 'Air-raid Shelter' sign.

How to make the living room

The second spread shows the interior of the living room. It might be useful for children to visit a museum with a wartime exhibition to get an impression of what home life was like.

1

Fold a piece of A5 paper diagonally and cut off the leftover strip.

2

Open the paper out and cut a small triangle from one creased corner.

3

Fold margins on the edges of the square, extending from the cut corner.

4

Fold on the diagonal and apply glue to the margins on the outside.

5

Lay the open sides of the triangle on the edges of the right page with the margin edge at the bottom. Close the page.

6

The floor pops up at the base of the page when opened.

How to make the living room furniture

A pop-up chair and a table set for tea finish off the living room. Once children have some practice at making these basic forms, they can be made more elaborate, for example by adding arms to the chair.

1

Cut a strip from the short edge of A5 paper.

2

Fold in half and fold back margins at the edges. Apply glue to the margins of the pop-up.

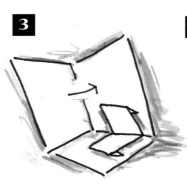

3

Lay the paper on the right page so that the centre fold lines up with the edge of floor. Close the book carefully.

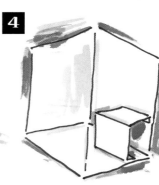

4

Open out and pull the table into pop-up position.

5

Take a narrower strip of paper and fold into quarters to form a chair.

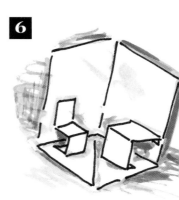

6

Position chair on the left page as shown and glue into place.

This is our main room. Dad used to sit in the big chair, but Grandma does now. We listen to the wireless constantly to hear about whats going on in the war. The gas mask holder is mine, because Judith, Grandma and Mum have gone out trying to get some more food from the green grocer's.

In the living room, Liz has drawn a wireless and a lino floor with a rug.

DESIGN TIPS

● Make folders to hold each child's bits and pieces.
● Make pop-up trial runs on odd paper.

How to make the Anderson shelter

The third spread shows the interior of the Anderson shelter. The floor is made as for the living room.

1

Cut a strip from the short edge of an A5 sheet.

2
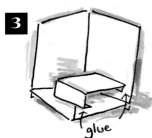
Fold margins on the short edges. Then fold 3 cm from the bottom margin.

3
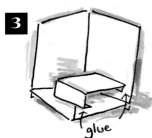
Glue the margin at the top of the bed into position on right page. Glue only the edge of the foot margin that touches the right triangle of the floor.

4
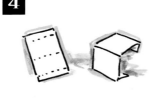
Make a smaller version of the living room table and attach it to the left page as a stool.

How to make the blitzed house

The fourth spread shows the exterior of the house after a bomb has hit it.

Make and attach the house as for the first spread, but cut down the shape to give the effect of a blitzed house.

The book ends dramatically with a bombing raid that leaves the house in flames.

The Anderson shelter looks quite cosy, with rugs and 'Home Sweet Home' sign.

31 · ALL MY OWN WORK

AIM: To review and promote books that the child has written, in a special pop-up leaflet.

PREPARATION: Children cut and folded the greetings card and constructed the origami book to go inside.

 Allow 2 hours.

How to use this project

This project provides children with a chance to look back at books they have made. First, discuss with the class the cover blurbs on books they are reading. Note the use of questions, enticing summaries and quotations from reviewers. The children then select either six books (one per page) or three books (one per spread) that they have made to review inside their mini pop-up book. The back and front pages of the pop-up are blank as these will be attached to the leaflet. Provide a framework for children to structure their book reviews around. For example, you could tell them to start with a quotation from the book, then summarise the story and finish with a quotation from a review. On the rest of the flyer, children write promotional copy, including an author profile.

Helia (age 11) used bright colours to highlight her copy.

How to make the leaflet

1

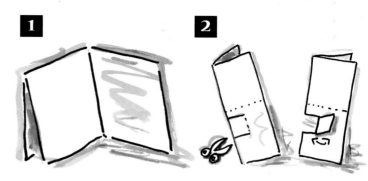

Fold A3 paper in quarters and unfold.

2

Fold the paper in half lengthways and make two parallel cuts in the bottom half, 6 cm deep and 10 cm apart. Fold and unfold.

3

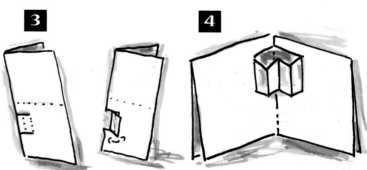

Fold the cut section in half and unfold.

4

Fold the paper into a greetings card and pull up the middle section as a zig-zag.

5

Make an origami book from A4 paper (see page 7).

6

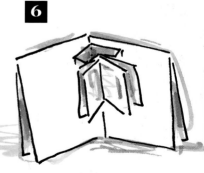

Glue the book into the middle of the pop-up so that it projects forwards.

PERSONAL
RECORD
BOOK

Title:

Author:

What I found hardest about making my book was

What I found easiest about making my book was

What I liked most about making my book was

I would like my next book to be about

What I liked least about making my book was

In my next book I need to improve